69
WAYS TO
PLEASE
YOUR
LOVER

DUNCAN BAIRD PUBLISHERS
LONDON

69 WAYS TO PLEASE YOUR LOVER

SEX SECRETS FOR ULTIMATE PLEASURE

NICOLE BAILEY

69 WAYS TO PLEASE YOUR LOVER

Nicole Bailey

Conceived, created and designed by
Duncan Baird Publishers Ltd
Sixth Floor
Castle House
75–76 Wells Street
London W1T 3QH

Managing Editor: Julia Charles
Editor: Ingrid Court-Jones
Designer: Manisha Patel
Commissioned Photography: John Davis

British Library Cataloguing-in-Publication Data:
A CIP record for this book is available from
the British Library

ISBN: 1-84483-001-2

10 9 8 7 6 5 4 3

Typeset in Futura Condensed

Printed by Regent, China

contents

the essence of pleasure

Whether you're reading this in bed with someone you've just met or your partner of ten years, *69 Ways to Please Your Lover* is for you. It's a guide to all the things that feel good during sex.

The first part is about techniques — it covers everything from playing to penetrating. The second part is a tour of the body's hot spots with tips on how to stimulate each one. The third part shows you how to hone each of your five senses so that sex becomes a rich and sensual pleasure trip that you experience not only through your genitals, but also through your nose, tongue, eyes and ears.

You don't need a perfect body to have good sex. Neither do you need a repertoire of flawless "moves". Often, all it takes is a sense of curiosity and the willingness to experiment. One couple I know revitalized their sex life by arranging afternoon "sex appointments" with each other. The results were startling – their sex life went from tepid to red hot in just days. Sex became their hobby. They surfed sex sites on the internet; they bought sex toys and books; and they even went on Tantric sex courses. They are living proof that pleasing your lover is a matter of attitude and enthusiasm. I hope that the tips and techniques included in this book will inspire, enrich and invigorate your sex life in exactly the same way. Have a good time reading and an even better time putting it all into practice!

introduction

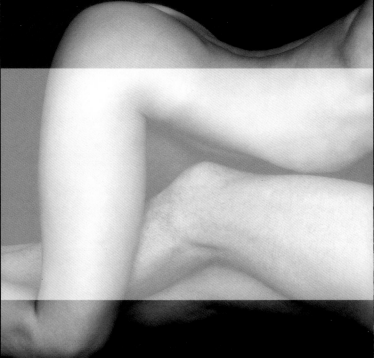

ACTIONS

fantasize • play • tickle • kiss • nibble • breathe • whisper • restrain •
lick • suck • penetrate

Some people say that the most important part of sex is not inter-course, but everything that you do beforehand — for example, the way in which you: whisper in your lover's ear, kiss their skin, go down on them, confess to an intimate sexual fantasy, nibble their neck or play sex games. These are the things that really seduce your lover, capture their imagination or take them by surprise. Part One is full of techniques and ideas intended to build up sexual tension notch by notch to create an erotic high for both of you. There are suggestions about how to make sex more playful (laughter and silliness are great ways to get rid of

inhibitions), enhance sensation using simple breathing techniques, rediscover passion through kissing, increase sexual
tension by using restraints and give each other fantastic oral sex.
You may even get so carried away that foreplay ends up as sex
in its own right. But of all the possible actions, the most crucial
one is communication — talking about sex together and asking
each other simple questions, such as "How does that feel?" can
be the single, most effective thing you can do to improve your
sex life. And when you talk about sex, don't forget that everyone loves receiving sexual compliments, so give generously!

Fantasies can really turn up the tempo during sex. They mean that your brain, as well as your body, is fully engaged in sex. It's like watching an erotic movie that you have written, directed and starred in — all in the privacy of your own mind. Fantasies can be about anything from a sexual encounter with a good-looking stranger to a ten-person orgy complete with bondage gear, whips and dildos. It's common to feel guilty about fantasizing or to worry about the content of our fantasies, but sex therapists

size

say we should just relax – as long as fantasies don't replace the desire to have sex with a lover or have a destructive effect on our lives, there's no problem. Fantasies are meant to be naughty – if they were clean, safe or mundane, they wouldn't have the power to turn us on. Some people are very creative when it comes to fantasies and have a vast repertoire of images and scenarios. Others find fantasies elusive. If the latter describes you, try treating yourself to a hot bath in which you

lize

fantasize

reminisce about your sexual experiences — the best, the worst, the funniest and the most adventurous. Which ones capture your imagination? Why? Find ways of embellishing your experiences or just zoom in on a particularly titillating detail — a fantasy can be something as simple as a single erotic snap-shot of someone's body. If your libido is jaded or you're finding it hard to get turned on because you're tired or stressed, conjuring up a favourite fantasy can give your arousal levels exactly the boost they need. Women who find it difficult to reach orgasm often report that creating larger-than-life sexual images in their head can tip them over the edge in a way that hours of skilled love-making can't. Where possible, try to close the gap between the sex that you fantasize about and the sex that you actually have in real life. So make love in the sea, meet in a hotel and pretend that you're strangers, act out kinky roles or strip for each other – follow whatever your imaginations dictate!

fantasize

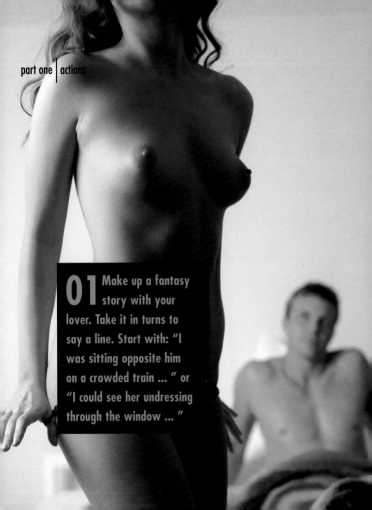

01 Make up a fantasy story with your lover. Take it in turns to say a line. Start with: "I was sitting opposite him on a crowded train ... " or "I could see her undressing through the window ... "

02 Act out a fantasy with your lover. Get the details just right – decorate the bedroom, use props or sex toys, dress up and use role play. Do whatever it takes to make your fantasy come to life.

"you show

Sex is playtime for adults. You can forget about obeying rules and, instead, be as naughty, dirty, adventurous or kinky as you like. Playful sex means expressing yourself in new, exciting and frequently silly ways. It could mean having sex in the garden at dusk and trying to be quiet so that the neighbours don't hear; it could be decorating her naked body with fruit; it could be drizzling honey along the length of his penis and refusing to suck it off until he talks dirty to you; or it could be greeting him at the front door, dressed in your sauciest underwear. Of course, playful sex would be incomplete without toys. If you don't want to visit a sex shop, go shopping online. The range of toys is enormous — as well as vibrators, dildos and bondage gear, it's also possible to buy silicone penis extensions, edible thongs, finger tinglers (vibrators that fit on your fingertips), strap-on clitoral stimulators, nipple jewelry — and "love swings" which are designed to be suspended from the ceiling for sex in mid-air.

03 Take some X-rated instant photos of yourself and leave them in places that will surprise your lover – in his wallet, in his jacket pocket or under his pillow when you leave in the morning.

04 Give your lover a shopping list for sexy foods such as asparagus, figs, oysters, bananas and whipped cream. At the end of your shopping list write, "Come back SOON."

05 Act out roles during sex. Call him "Sir" or "Lord" and call her "Madam" or "Lady". Pretend that she's an innocent virgin or that he's a repressed headmaster in need of liberation.

tingling

anticip

Imagine lying on your front with your eyes closed and your lover kneeling beside you. You know that any second he is going to tickle your back with a feather. The skin all over your body is alive and tingling with anticipation. Tickling wakes you up, energizes you and makes you feel like you're really inside your body. The sexiest type of tickle creates a feeling that is half turn-on, half shiver. The best tools for tickling are your hands. Lie down and get your lover to gently drag their fingertips or

tickle

fingernails across large expanses of your skin. Alternatively, leave a tiny space between your fingertips and their skin – this produces sensations that are literally hair-raising. Other good tickling tools include your hair (especially if it's long and fine), silk scarves and feathers or feather dusters. Tickling is all about creating a sense of expectation in your lover and you can heighten this by blind-folding them, which will make them focus even more keenly on their sense of touch.

06 Ask your lover to put on her tightest jeans and then use your fingers to tickle the inside of her thigh and her crotch. The thicker the fabric of the jeans, the harder you can tickle.

07 Gather together some brushes that have different-textured bristles. Blindfold your partner and then treat them to a sensual feast by gently brushing their skin all over.

mouth t

O f all the sexual acts, kissing is the most intimate and emotionally charged. An electrifying

kiss on the mouth that lasts just seconds can have

you begging your lover for sex in a way that an

hour of stroking and cuddling often can't. A kiss is

the first sexual impression we have of a lover and it

can make or break the desire for more intimacy.

The best type of kiss is one which you want to con-

tinue indefinitely. You pace yourselves to match the

intensity of the mood: starting off slow, teasing and

tongue t

kiss

tentative and becoming more urgent and passionate as the sexual tension mounts. Neither partner
feels dominated or dominating. This type of kiss can
be an end in itself rather than a part of foreplay.
Hot kissing is an essential way to keep the sexual
buzz alive in relationships so, if you've been with
your lover a long time and have become lazy about
kissing, it's time to do some revision. Ask your lover
to kiss you in the way that they have always longed
to be kissed, then lie back and take note!

o tongue

08 Try "conscious kissing" in which you focus 100 per cent on the sensation of kissing – the taste, the feel, the smell of your partner's mouth, lips and tongue. Be completely in the moment.

09 Kiss like teenagers: on the street, in the back row of the cinema or in the bedroom. But above all, kiss for a long time. Don't think about what happens next – kiss for the pure pleasure of it.

soft an

The all-time expert on bites and nibbles is Vatsyayana, author of the *Kama Sutra*. He classified bites according to where and how the teeth marks were made. For example, "the 'bite of the boar' is imprinted on the breasts and the shoulders, and consists of two lines of teeth marks." Vatsyayana also described how lovers used biting to communicate passion. "If she is very excited ... she will take him by the hair, pull his head toward her and bite his lower lip, then in her delirium she will

d hard

bite him all over his body." Although less fashion-able these days, biting can be an interesting sexual technique. How much you and your lover enjoy it will depend on your levels of pain tolerance. Gently nibbling ears, fingers and toes can up the erotic tempo in seconds whereas hard bites can be a instant passion killer (unless, of course, you're into S&M). A good technique is to suck your lover's flesh into your mouth, then gently nibble it – try this on the buttock or the inner arm.

nibble

10 Massage his erect penis with oil and take it into your mouth. Use your teeth to gently graze the skin along the length of his shaft. Ask him to tell you if he'd like it harder or softer.

11 Rest your upper teeth on the top of the web between your thumb and index finger and your tongue on the bottom. Now pull your hand away. Try the same thing on her inner labia.

12 Gently draw some of your lover's flesh into your mouth, lightly "secure" it with your teeth and now just breathe in and out so that your warm breath caresses their skin.

sigh p

One of the easiest but most overlooked ways to enhance sex is by using your breath. Yogis and Tantric sex masters have always known this, and breathing exercises form a core part of Tantric sex workshops. The principle is simple: how you feel — physically and emotionally — is closely related to how you breathe. Practising a simple breathing exercise with your lover before sex is a wonderful way to feel more centred. People often have sex late at night when they are tired — by taking a couple of minutes to gather yourself you will able to make love in a more attentive and enjoyable way. Start by sitting cross-legged facing each other. Look into each others' eyes and hold hands. Alternatively, you can place your palm on your lover's chest, around their heart area. Observe the quality of your breathing – is it smooth or ragged, deep or shallow? Gradually make a conscious effort to slow it down and make it deeper and smoother. Now synchronize your breath with your lover's so that your

breathe

ant gasp

in- and out-breaths are the same length and texture. Imagine that your breathing connects you to each other and brings you closer emotionally. Do this exercise for at least two minutes. You can also use your breath during sex to delay or encourage orgasm or even to make your climax more intense. To delay orgasm, take long, slow, deep breaths and relax your body and mind (this is great for men who ejaculate too soon). To encourage orgasm, take fast, deep breaths that flood the whole body with oxygen

rhythm

breathe

(great for women who find climax elusive). To make your orgasms more intense, hold your breath during the build-up to orgasm, then at the critical moment release it in a long, loud "ahhhh" sound. Some people also find that short, sharp panting breaths before orgasm can enhance sensation. After sex connect with your lover by lying in the spoons position and synchronizing breathing. Put your hands on each other's bellies to feel the rhythm of the breath as it enters and leaves your bodies.

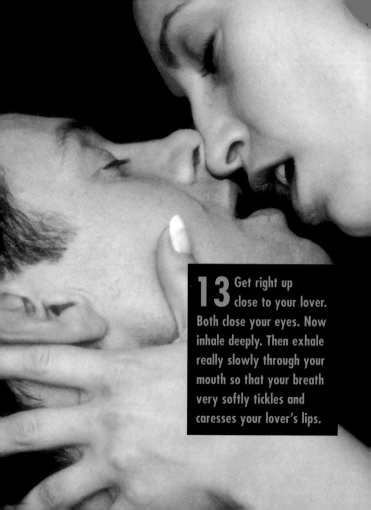

13 Get right up close to your lover. Both close your eyes. Now inhale deeply. Then exhale really slowly through your mouth so that your breath very softly tickles and caresses your lover's lips.

14 Try "sensual breathing" during sex. Breathe in deeply, down to the bottom of your lungs. As you do so, imagine that the air is pushing erotic sensations around your body.

15 This is the most intimate breathing of all: put your lips against those of your lover to make an airtight seal. Now gently breathe each other's breath.

"I...Really...

Don't just say it to your lover — whisper it. It doesn't matter whether you're alone in bed together or at a party full of people, whispering to your lover says "I've got something very private to tell you." A whisper excludes everyone and everything else and draws you and your lover into your own erotic universe. Try looking her in the eye and saying "I need to tell you something." Then lean close to her ear, pause, and say in your slowest and breathiest whisper, "I ... really ... want ... you."

The sensation of hot breath against her skin and the message of urgent passion can be incredibly seductive. Now it's over to her ... A whisper is also a good way of getting close to a desirable stranger. Speaking to a stranger in a loud voice says "I'm desperate to get your attention." Speaking to them in a soft voice says "I'm confident that you're going to listen." But whispering conveys true sexual confidence – the subtext is: "I fancy you and I'm going to make you move closer to me."

whisper

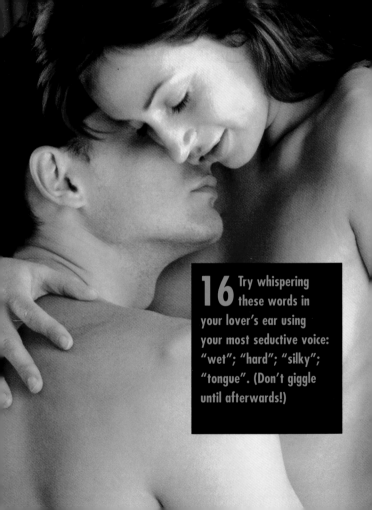

16 Try whispering these words in your lover's ear using your most seductive voice: "wet"; "hard"; "silky"; "tongue". (Don't giggle until afterwards!)

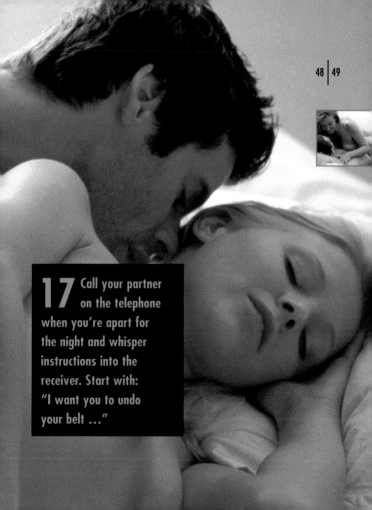

17 Call your partner on the telephone when you're apart for the night and whisper instructions into the receiver. Start with: "I want you to undo your belt …"

Whether you enjoy being tied to the bedposts
with silk scarves or you prefer leather straps,
chains and handcuffs, there can be something
amazingly liberating about bondage. It can turn
conservative lovers into avid fetishists or brazen
dominatrices. While the restrainer gets a powerful
kick out of being in charge, the restrainee gets to
experience a naughty-but-nice fear of degradation.
So if you're the boss, tie up your "victim" using soft
cord, scarves or ties – or professional bondage gear

rves

restrain

if you've got it – then play up your role to the max. Tell your "victim" how naughty they have been and how their "punishment" will be to obey all your sexual commands. Alternatively, punish them by arousing them and then withdrawing all stimulation until it suits you to continue. Some couples like to establish a code word before they start playing bondage games so that they can call a halt at any time. But don't choose the word "stop", because shouting this is all part of the fun.

straps

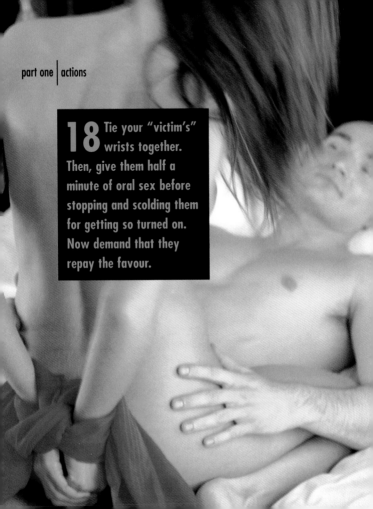

18 Tie your "victim's" wrists together. Then, give them half a minute of oral sex before stopping and scolding them for getting so turned on. Now demand that they repay the favour.

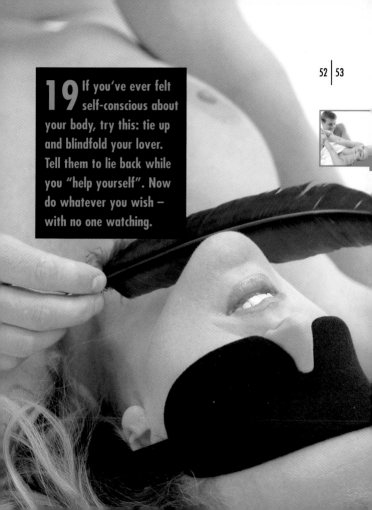

19 If you've ever felt self-conscious about your body, try this: tie up and blindfold your lover. Tell them to lie back while you "help yourself". Now do whatever you wish – with no one watching.

long, slow, broa

The tongue can be one of the most provocative parts of the body. It's also incredibly adaptable in terms of shape and movement. You can use it in different ways on different parts of your lover's body. For example, you can flick the tip across the nipples, you can use the flat of your tongue to maximize tongue-to-genital contact or you can make your tongue alternately soft and swirling, then hard and penetrating on the entrance to the vagina. Alex Comfort, author of *The Joy of Sex*, recommends the

lick

"tongue bath", in which you systematically lick your lover's entire body with "long, slow, broad tongue strokes". You can also create exquisite sensations by licking your lover's erogenous zones and then gently blowing warm air on their wet skin. Explore with your tongue – licking someone's ear can drive them to ecstasy while licking the soft skin behind their knees will take them by surprise. If you want your lover to lick you, lure them with dabs of honey or flavoured lubricant applied in strategic places.

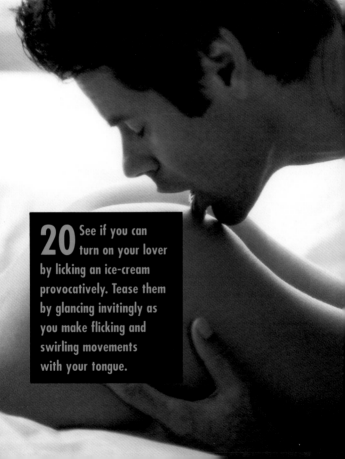

20 See if you can turn on your lover by licking an ice-cream provocatively. Tease them by glancing invitingly as you make flicking and swirling movements with your tongue.

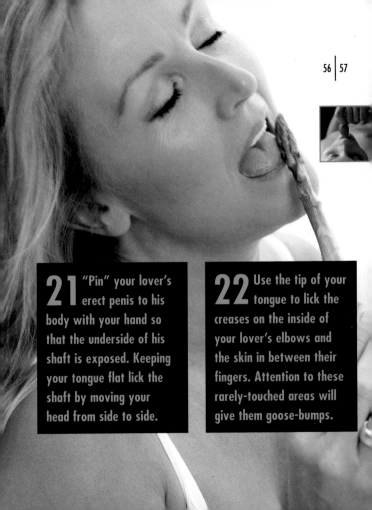

21 "Pin" your lover's erect penis to his body with your hand so that the underside of his shaft is exposed. Keeping your tongue flat lick the shaft by moving your head from side to side.

22 Use the tip of your tongue to lick the creases on the inside of your lover's elbows and the skin in between their fingers. Attention to these rarely-touched areas will give them goose-bumps.

teeth

to

If you enjoy provocative come-ons, try sucking a lollipop while gazing suggestively into your lover's eyes. The message is clear: "Come here and let me suck you too!" Sucking on parts of the body, such as fingers, toes, nipples and genitals, can be an orgasmic experience. The trick is to use your teeth, tongue and lips all at once to create multi-layered sensations. But don't suck your lover's neck unless you want to cover them with lurid love bites. While the majority of men love to have their penis sucked, some women find direct clitoral sucking too intense, unless they are at the very peak of arousal – if in doubt, ask first. Sucking is a good way to give him an erection when you've had sex a couple of times and his penis is flagging. Put your lips around the base of his shaft, making an air-tight seal. Now suck as hard as you can for as long as you can (don't forget to breathe through your nose!). This strong sucking creates a vacuum that causes blood to rush into the penis and make it go hard.

ngue

suck

lips

23 Use your front teeth to gently push back the clitoral hood to expose the tip of the clitoris. Suck the clitoris to draw it out. Still sucking, flick it fast from left to right with your tongue.

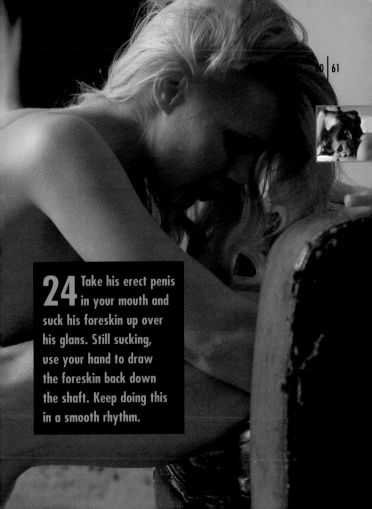

24 Take his erect penis in your mouth and suck his foreskin up over his glans. Still sucking, use your hand to draw the foreskin back down the shaft. Keep doing this in a smooth rhythm.

Penetration — you can do it standing, sitting, lying down, side-by-side, head-to-toe or face-to-face. The variations are endless. Sex gets boring if you always do it in the same way, so be creative. Women: to stimulate your G-spot lie on your back with him inside you, then put your feet flat on his chest. Or, savour the feeling of penetration without movement by getting on top of him and, once he's inside you, lie back and rest your head between his feet. Men: to enjoy deep penetration face-to-face, get her to straddle you as you sit back on your heels. Or, if you love rear penetration, ask her to squat down with her hands on the floor and then straighten her legs so that she's in a semi-standing position, facing away from you. If you are both happiest making love in the missionary position, add some interesting variations, such as letting your head hang off the side of the bed, raising her hips with pillows or rolling over (still joined) mid-way through to give her chance to be on top.

penetrate

25 Tease her by barely penetrating her for the first five strokes of intercourse. Then, on the sixth stroke, thrust all the way inside her. Do five more shallow strokes and then a deep one, and so on.

26 Why not try experimenting with improvised edible dildos, such as cucumbers and bananas? (Make sure that they're squeaky clean first though.)

27 Put a blindfold on him and caress him. Don't let him enter you until you think he is close to orgasm. Then guide him inside you in such a way that your genitals are the only parts of you touching.

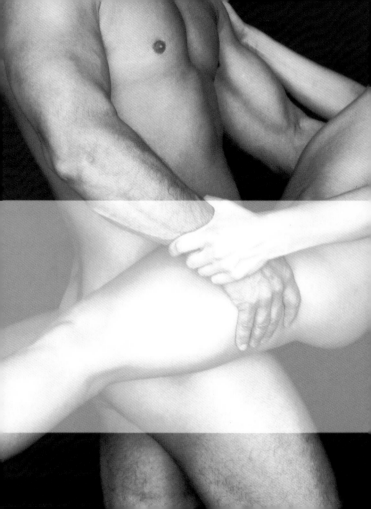

PART TWO

HOT SPOTS

ear • mouth • neck • breast • navel • clitoris • g-spot • penis • balls •
buttocks • toe

The undisputed hot spots of the male and female body are the penis and the clitoris. These are the epicentres of sensual and erotic pleasure, and, given the right stimulation, they can transport you into a state of ecstasy. But many people say that they would love more attention to be paid to the rest of their bodies – that instead of making a beeline for the genitals they would enjoy it if their lovers made love to other areas of their body first, especially the parts that are often neglected or given only cursory attention. If your sex life always consists of kissing, followed by touching each other's genitals, followed by intercourse,

hot spots

try changing the emphasis — instead of concentrating exclusively on the parts of the body that will bring you to orgasm, turn sex into a long, meandering voyage of discovery in which you both spend time just touching. The suggestions in this part of the book encourage you to explore the whole of each other — from the ears to the navel to the toes. If you have an orgasm in the process, fine. But if you don't, that's fine too. The advantage of making sex an all-body experience is that it slows things down and gives you chance to get really aroused, so that if you do then have intercourse the sensations are explosive!

The ear is so sensitive that some people can have an orgasm from ear stimulation or "aural sex" alone. This "auriculogenital reflex" is attributed to a nerve in the auditory canal. If your lover dissolves when you nuzzle their ears, try the following strokes which are based on Indian head massage techniques. Ask your lover to close their eyes. Stand behind them and place your palms (which should be warm) over their ears for a few seconds. Gently move your palms in slow circles — ask your lover to concentrate on the sound that this makes and to block out all other thoughts. Make light pinching or circular movements along the ear flap, from the top of the ear right down to the tip of the lobe and back again. Now insert the tips of your forefingers into the ears so that they rest just on (but not *in*) the opening of the auditory canal. Softly rotate your forefingers on the openings. Finish by covering your lover's ears with your palms again. By now their ears should be hot, red and tingling.

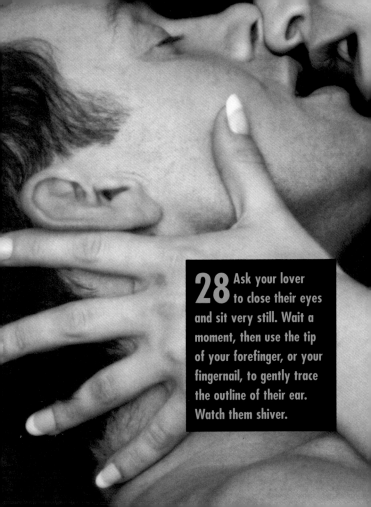

28 Ask your lover to close their eyes and sit very still. Wait a moment, then use the tip of your forefinger, or your fingernail, to gently trace the outline of their ear. Watch them shiver.

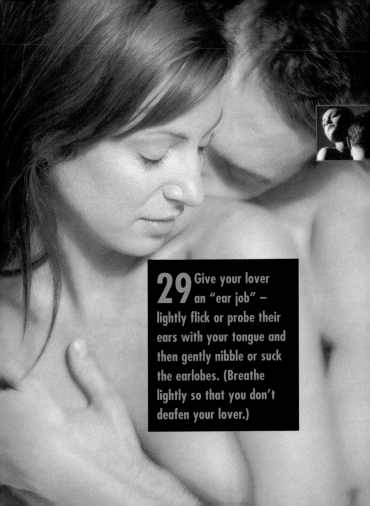

29 Give your lover an "ear job" – lightly flick or probe their ears with your tongue and then gently nibble or suck the earlobes. (Breathe lightly so that you don't deafen your lover.)

The mouth is an extremely versatile sex organ: you can use it to lick, enclose, suck, nuzzle, blow, kiss, nibble and bite. If you want to find out just how versatile it is, try making love with nothing but your mouth. The combination of red lips and soft, pink tongue make the mouth seem made for sex. Anthropologists say that we paint our lips or pierce our tongues to draw attention to them. In some cultures it's still common practice to enlarge the lower lip by inserting a plate into it or to

lick

decorate the mouth by inserting "plugs" of metal, ivory or bone. Some lovers express intimacy by exchanging food or drink with their mouths. This was turned into an erotic art in the film *Tampopo* – two lovers slid a raw egg yolk suggestively back and forth between their mouths until the climactic moment when the yolk burst. If you don't fancy egg yolk, try trickling cold champagne from your mouth into your lover's, or giving them a soft fruit, such as a lychee, cherry or grape with your teeth.

nibble

bite

mouth

30 Slowly and gently trace your forefinger around the outline of your lover's lips. Then, kiss your lover on the incredibly sensitive points at the corners of their mouth.

31 Take your lover's right thumb in your mouth and use your lips, teeth and tongue to give it a mini-blow job. Do this to each finger on their right hand. Now give their left hand the same treatment.

32 Massage your lover's lip. Use the tips of both forefingers to apply gentle, static pressure first along the length of their top lip and then along their bottom lip.

nuzz

nibb

Necks, like ears and toes, respond to sensual touch by sending waves of pleasure rippling through the rest of the body. Sucking, nuzzling or nibbling the neck can be a fast-track to sexual arousal. And, if your lover is feeling tense, a neck massage is a fantastic way to help them unwind and feel languorous and sexy. Put one hand on your lover's head and with your other hand spread your fingers and thumb across the base of their neck. Slide your hand to the top of their neck and then firmly grasp the flesh and pull away. Do the same thing half way down the neck and then again at the base of the neck. This feels (and smells) especially good if your fingers are coated with coconut oil. If you like, you can extend the neck massage to the scalp – plant your fingertips firmly on the head and then move your hands in slow circles (your finger-tips stay still – only the scalp moves). Try to breathe in harmony with each other. This simple massage can take some people into another dimension.

33 If you have long fingernails, rest them on his hairline at the top of his neck and then very gently drag them down the length of his neck. The effect is spine-tingling.

34 There are three hot spots on the neck: the nape, the curve where the neck meets the shoulder and the underside of the jaw. Plant a line of featherlight kisses in all three places.

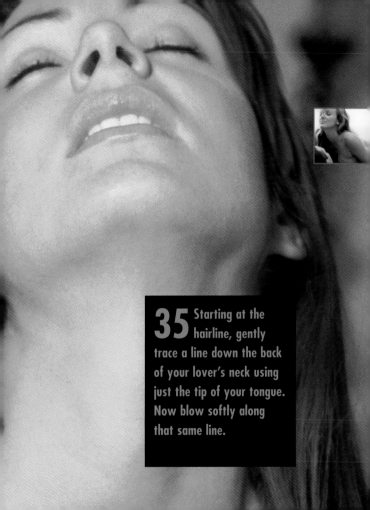

35 Starting at the hairline, gently trace a line down the back of your lover's neck using just the tip of your tongue. Now blow softly along that same line.

Women often complain that, although men pay lip service (literally!) to their breasts, they don't give this erogenous zone enough attention. Despite the fact that women vary in nipple sensitivity, many say that there is a hot wire between their nipples and their clitoris and that it's possible to have an orgasm from breast stimulation alone. If this describes your lover, try dedicating a whole sex session to making love to just her breasts. Trace circles around her nipples using your wet fingers, the

breast

tip of your tongue or the lubricated tip of your penis. Gently tweak and suck her nipples, kiss and knead her breasts and nuzzle the places where each breast joins her body. If her breasts are large enough to meet, you can try a practice known as coitus *à mammilla* – she uses her hands to "wrap" her breasts around the shaft of your penis and then you thrust between them. Women with large breasts can do this lying on their back; women with smaller breasts find it easier when on top.

36 Play "hot and cold" with your lover's nipples. First, suck them in your warm mouth, then rub them with ice cubes. Now breathe hot air on them before you take them in your mouth again.

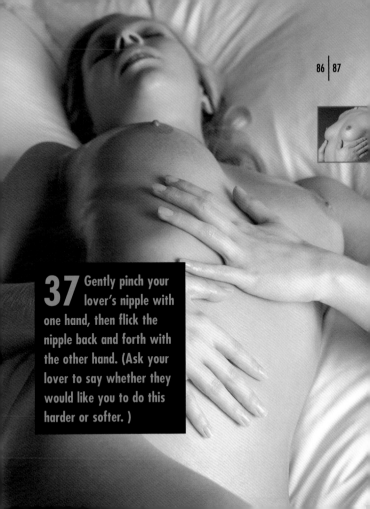

37 Gently pinch your lover's nipple with one hand, then flick the nipple back and forth with the other hand. (Ask your lover to say whether they would like you to do this harder or softer.)

The navel is sexy because it resembles the labia and vaginal opening in shape – anthropologists describe it as a "genital echo". Lots of people show off their navel by piercing or decorating it. Although this part of the body is an erogenous zone for some, others find stimulation here too ticklish. Try exploring your lover's navel with your fingers and tongue – if they don't like navel penetration, use the fingertips of your index and middle finger to stretch the navel into a closed slit and lick around its edges. There's an area in women about one hand-width below the navel, immediately above the pubic bone, which can yield fantastic sensations. Wait until she's really aroused, preferably at the point of climax, and then press your palm down firmly on this area while simultaneously stimulating her clitoris or G-spot. Ask her to tell you how hard to press (if she's still able to speak!). As an alternative, you can use a vibrator instead of your palm. This technique is a good way to intensify her orgasm.

navel

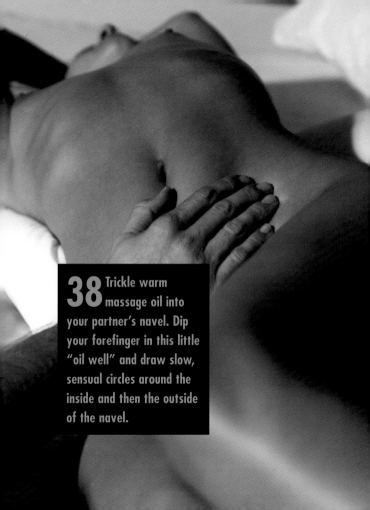

38 Trickle warm massage oil into your partner's navel. Dip your forefinger in this little "oil well" and draw slow, sensual circles around the inside and then the outside of the navel.

39 Make love to her navel with your tongue by darting it up and down, from side to side and round and round. At the same time stimulate her clitoris or G-spot with your fingertips.

suck

rub

The clitoris has been called a "bud", a "bean", a "dot" and a "joy button" — all names that give the impression that it's something small. In fact, it's huge — although you can only see the little pink tip (the glans), the clitoris extends back into the body to form a large network of tissues (feel the shaft of the clitoris as a firm, movable cord underneath the clitoral hood). And when she's turned on, this tissue gets erect in exactly the same way as the penis. There's a lot of mystique about the clitoris and how to touch it. Try gently sucking the tip, flicking your tongue from side to side or up and down, or using your fingers to tickle or rub the clitoral hood in circles or figures of eight. And try putting your fingers or a vibrator in her vagina at the same time – lots of women say they like the "full" feeling that this creates. When you rub her clitoris, ask her for instructions such as "faster", "slower", "harder" or "softer" – and rest assured that if you're doing it right you'll know by her expression.

clitoris

stroke

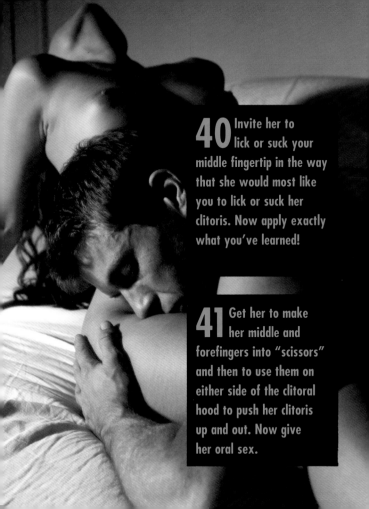

40 Invite her to lick or suck your middle fingertip in the way that she would most like you to lick or suck her clitoris. Now apply exactly what you've learned!

41 Get her to make her middle and forefingers into "scissors" and then to use them on either side of the clitoral hood to push her clitoris up and out. Now give her oral sex.

42 Ask her to gently pull up her pubic hair toward her navel during missionary-position sex. This movement makes her vulva taut as well as exposing her clitoris for maximum stimulation.

"don't

The "G" in "G-spot" stands for Grafenburg, the name of the German gynecologist who first located this fabled erogenous zone. There are many misunderstandings about the G-spot. Does it really exist? Where exactly is it? Does every woman have one? Because the G-spot is hidden away inside the vagina, many women are unsure about what it is exactly and what it does. By far the quickest way to discover the truth is to get down there with your lover and explore your own G-spot. Try this

stop

now"

technique: hold your first and second fingers in the air and bend them into a beckoning position. Now keep your fingers in this position and insert them into your vagina. Aim to get your fingertips to touch the front vaginal wall about 5 cm (2 in) up inside. Feel around for a bumpy or raised patch that produces interesting sensations when touched. In medical terms, this is an area of spongy tissue that surrounds your urethra (the tube by which urine leaves your body). When you hit the right spot you

g-spot

may feel like you want to pee; or you may feel a deep, growing sense of pleasure; or then again you may feel nothing at all! It helps if you're already aroused before you start searching for your G-spot. If it's hard to get your fingers in the right place, get your lover to do it or try out some vibrators that have been specially designed to stimulate the G-spot — they look like standard vibrators but have a bent or curved tip. Many women say that the best type of G-spot stimulation is deep, static pressure or firm

nse

stroking rather than light tickling. It's important to know that G-spot feelings are highly personal and there is a wide scale of response, ranging from complete indifference to intense orgasm. Although you might be disappointed if you experience little or no response, you are certainly neither strange nor unusual. On the other hand, if you're lucky enough to have discovered G-spot bliss, go one step further by getting your lover to stimulate your G-spot and clitoris at the same time.

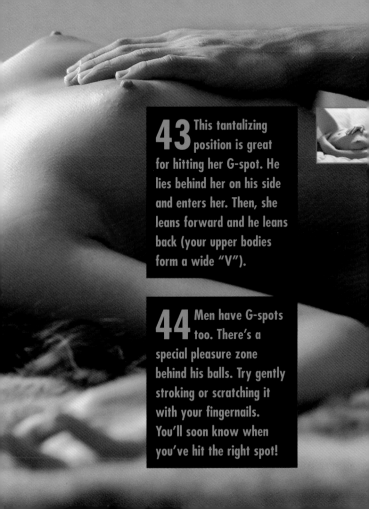

43 This tantalizing position is great for hitting her G-spot. He lies behind her on his side and enters her. Then, she leans forward and he leans back (your upper bodies form a wide "V").

44 Men have G-spots too. There's a special pleasure zone behind his balls. Try gently stroking or scratching it with your fingernails. You'll soon know when you've hit the right spot!

The hot spot on the penis is known as the F-spot. F is for frenulum – the membrane on the underside of the shaft where the foreskin joins the penis. When you go down on your lover, spend lots of time flicking and whirling your tongue on this sensitive spot. Alternatively, take his glans in your mouth and then insert your index finger or thumb between your lips so that you can caress his F-spot manually. Many men fantasize about "deep throat" – an oral sex technique in which you take his entire penis into

your mouth and throat. Women find this difficult, because when the penis hits the back of the throat it stimulates the gag reflex. As an alternative to deep throat, try taking his penis as far into your mouth as is comfortable (easiest if you sit astride him facing his feet) and then either hum or gulp — he'll feel as though he's being swallowed. If you prefer to use your hands to bring your lover to orgasm, ask if you can watch him masturbate. Even if you've watched before, make sure that this time

penis

you really observe the details. Note whether he uses one hand or two, the position of his hand(s), the speed of his strokes, and what he likes to use as a lubricant. Now it's your go. Make sure you use lots of lubricant so that your fingers slide and glide over his shaft. If you want to experiment with your own strokes at the beginning, that's fine — just remember to use fast, rhythmic and familiar strokes toward the end. Then find out what he likes immediately after he's climaxed. Some men feel

slide al

incredibly sensitive after ejaculation and want you to let go fast; others enjoy having their penis held. If you really want to indulge your lover, buy him a sex toy. Although plenty of women have experimented with vibrators, it's often a novel experience for a man to feel high-speed friction on his penis. You can use a standard vibrator, but even better are the vibrators specifically designed for men. You put them over the head of the penis, or around the base or shaft – then you just switch them on.

penis

d glide

45 Give him a "quiet" blow job. Lie facing each other on your sides, your mouth level with his penis. Take him in your mouth, but stay completely still and quiet — let him do all the thrusting.

46 Enclose his erect penis in your oiled fists (one fist on top of the other). Now twist them in opposite directions as if you're wringing out a cloth. Twirl your tongue on his glans at the same time.

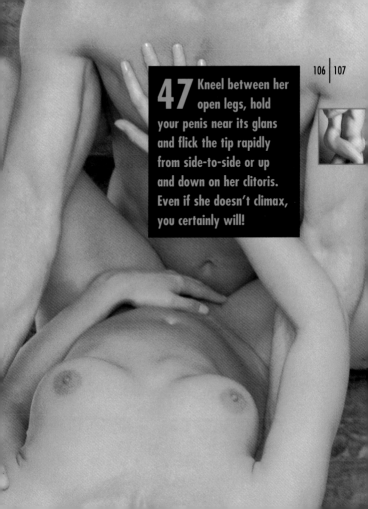

47 Kneel between her open legs, hold your penis near its glans and flick the tip rapidly from side-to-side or up and down on her clitoris. Even if she doesn't climax, you certainly will!

Men love having their balls held, especially during masturbation and oral sex. To perfect your "ball-hold", use one hand to cup both balls in your palm while using the other hand to encircle the top of the scrotal sac with your thumb and forefinger. The best position in which to do this is with him standing and you kneeling — this way you can use your lips and tongue to lick, nuzzle and suck his balls too. Men who enjoy lots of mouth-and-ball play sometimes shave their balls so that the skin of the

balls

scrotum is baby smooth and kissable. If you want

to try shaving your balls, make sure that you do

it when the scrotal skin is completely relaxed –

say, after a hot bath. For men who come too soon

during sex, there's a great testicle technique that

can help to prolong intercourse. When you're feel-

ing hyper-aroused and close to orgasm, just reach

down and tug firmly on your scrotum (or get your

lover to do it). This action should delay the point of

no return for at least a minute or two.

48 Try taking both his balls in your mouth and sucking them. Get him to kneel over your face, then encircle the top of his balls with your thumb and forefinger and gently guide them into your mouth.

49 Give him a special treat by taking his balls gently into your mouth and humming! This creates a tantalizing, warm sensation in the testicles by making them vibrate.

Stroking, scratching, nibbling or kneading the buttocks can drive some people crazy. Try giving your lover a buttock massage – coat the backs of your hands in oil and then use your fists to apply deep, static pressure to the centre of each buttock. Now twist your wrists so that your fists move in half circles. Make up your own massage strokes – drag your fingernails lightly across the buttocks, walk your index and middle fingers from the top of the buttock to the bottom, use the sides of your hands in hacking strokes or, if your partner likes it, try some light spanking. If your partner really enjoys spanking, you can invest in a leather or fur paddle that is designed specifically for this use. For some, the appeal of the buttocks is visual — tight, compact lines or full, voluptuous curves. If he's a buttock fan, exploit this fully by wearing g-strings and tight jeans, and by making love in the "doggy" position. Or, if touching his firm buttocks turns you on, give him a buttock massage while you are having sex.

buttocks

50 Coat your hands in massage oil and rub them all over her buttocks to create a slick surface. Now get her to lie down on her front and thrust your penis against her buttocks.

51 Next time you're in the throes of a deep, passionate kiss with your lover, reach behind him, put your hands on his buttocks and pull him vigorously toward you.

52 If she gets really turned on by having her buttocks caressed, try increasing her pleasure by using your other hand to explore her vagina or to stimulate her clitoris at the same time.

The feet are one of the most sensually neglected parts of the body – they're also very sensitive. This means that when you do "go down" on your lover's toes it feels nothing less than thrilling. The secret of a good toe job is to start off in the bath. Sit at opposite ends and give him a soapy foot massage. Now dry his feet with a warm towel and invite him into the bedroom. Get him to lie on his back with you at his feet so that he can see what you're doing. Coat your hands in massage oil, rub them toe

together and now just enclose the main part of his foot in both hands firmly for about half a minute (try this on yourself to discover how good it feels). Next, take his big toe into your mouth and suck it hard. At the same time, slip your oiled index finger in and out of the space between his big toe and second toe. Do this in between each toe in turn. Add your own personal touches, such as lightly nibbling the top of each toe or moving your mouth up and down on each toe while making eye contact.

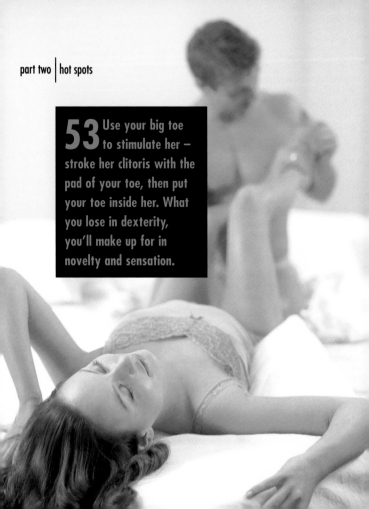

53 Use your big toe to stimulate her – stroke her clitoris with the pad of your toe, then put your toe inside her. What you lose in dexterity, you'll make up for in novelty and sensation.

54 Slide your toes up and down his penis and then apply firm pressure to his perineum with your heel. In Tantric sex the pleasure centre in the perineum is known as the "sacred spot".

55 Give your lover a novel experience – use a vibrator to massage the delicate and very sensitive places in between their toes.

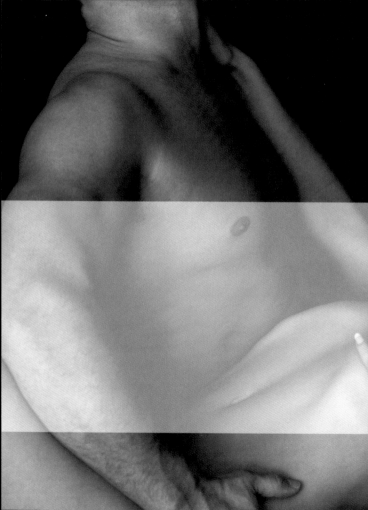

PART THREE

SENSATION

touch • taste • sight • smell • sound

shut out the rest of the world and concentrate exclusively on each other's bodies. Sex therapists often say that the root of their clients' problems is that they have sex "in their heads rather than in their bodies". In other words, people think too much during sex. They are too busy having an internal dialogue about how they're feeling – or how they think their partner is feeling – to give themselves up to pure physical sensation. Great sex happens when your mind is allowed to take a back seat and you exist solely in the realm of your senses. This is easier said than

sensation

done – our senses are often dulled by day-to-day life and we have to work hard to reawaken them. This is where the technique of mindfulness comes in useful. Mindfulness is the ability to be completely absorbed or "present" in the moment. For example, to eat an orange mindfully would involve being conscious of nothing but the sensory experience of the orange in your mouth – its taste, smell and texture. The suggestions in this part of the book are designed to help you become more mindful – to explore touch, taste, sight, smell and sound – so that you can start to experience sex in a very physical way.

touch

right

Sometimes we're so obsessed with reaching orgasm that we forget how to really touch each other. To rediscover this lost art, start by collecting items that you find sensual — for example, silk cloth or fake fur. Then, give your lover a massage using not only your hands, but also your elbows, arms, feet and lips, and any of the sensual items you collected. Experiment all over their body with different pressures, strokes and speeds. After the massage, ask your lover what they enjoyed most and build on this. You can make your massage even more sensual by guiding your lover through a visualization beforehand. Ask them to imagine that they're about to have a massage, after having been deprived of touch for a long time. Get them to focus on their lower back and imagine how lovely it would feel if this area were the first to be touched. Can they make the skin of their lower back shiver and tingle in anticipation? Can they make the skin of other parts of their body react in this way?

me there"

touch

56 Exploit the body's sensitivity to temperature by having a hot bath with your lover in which you spray her feet with cold water. Or place a warm washcloth over his penis after orgasm.

57 Use familiar objects to touch each other in novel ways. For example, ask her to get down on all fours and then draw a silk scarf or a string of beads back and forth across her genitals.

Some tastes are naturally sexy. It may be the rich, decadent flavour of dark chocolate (itself a reputed aphrodisiac) or the fizzy fruitiness of champagne. Or it could be the salty tang of the sea that comes from oysters or caviar. Some people even say that eating food spiced with ginger or chilli inflames their senses. Whatever food turns you on, make a meal out of it. Dispense with cutlery and feed your lover with your fingers. Some lovers enjoy eating off each others' bodies — try arranging a feast on your

taste

lover's naked belly. Choose foods that are sticky, sweet, creamy or juicy. Of course, the real taste of sex comes directly from your lover – no food can compare to the sensual familiarity of your lover's mouth, skin or genitals. If you feel reticent about oral sex because you are worried about how you taste, remind yourself that genital secretions contain natural aphrodisiacs. Men can make their semen taste sweeter by abstaining from cigarettes, coffee and beer and by eating fruit, such as kiwis.

58 Add an interesting zing to intercourse by getting him to use peppermint-flavoured penis balm. Alternatively, try sucking a menthol sweet just before you give oral sex.

59 Say "You taste gorgeous," next time you go down on your lover. You'll not only help them to relax, but you'll also boost their self-confidence and make them feel incredibly sexy.

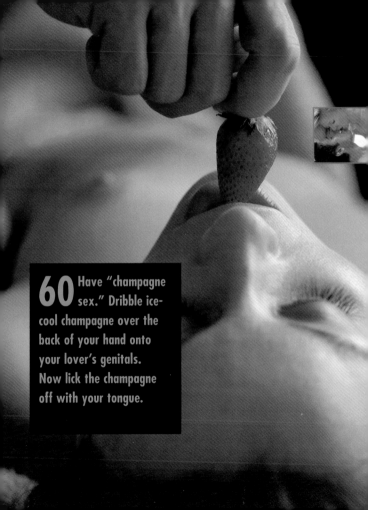

60 Have "champagne sex." Dribble ice-cool champagne over the back of your hand onto your lover's genitals. Now lick the champagne off with your tongue.

Sexual attraction often begins with sight. When you first meet your lover, you drink in their every physical detail — the way they stand, walk, sit and smile and the clothes they wear. Even their tiniest facial expression is fascinating. But once you're familiar with your lover, these heightened powers of observation disappear. One way to change this is to practise "mindful looking". This means being completely present in the moment and learning about your lover's body using the sense of sight. Start by getting into a meditative state of mind by, say,

practising yoga or t'ai chi or having a relaxing

bath. Then, take time to simply gaze at each other's

faces and bodies (if this makes either of you

uncomfortable, combine it with a massage). As you

look, concentrate on details, such as the shape of

the lips, the texture of the skin, or the curve of the

hips. Imagine that you're not going to see your

lover for a long time and you need to etch their

body and face indelibly in your memory.

ction

sight

61 This sex therapy exercise increases intimacy and boosts self-confidence. Stand naked in front of a mirror with your lover. Now point out what you really love about each other's bodies.

62 Practise soul-gazing during sex by looking deep into each other's eyes right up to and during orgasm – you'll feel an amazing sense of connection.

63 Watch a sexy movie together. Or try looking at some beautiful, sensual art, such as the *Kama Sutra*, or erotic Japanese prints or illustrations from Chinese pillow books.

perfume of h

Many of us spend so much time washing and deodorizing ourselves that by the time we get into bed all our natural smells have vanished. The truth is that bodily smells are a powerful turn-on because they contain chemicals called pheromones — nature's aphrodisiacs. As Alex Comfort, author of *The Joy of Sex*, says "Her perfume can be a long-range weapon (nothing seduces a man more reliably ...)". Discover the animal power of smell — instead of washing before sex, take a "scent tour" of each other's bodies. Explore each other's genitals, nipples, navels and armpits — each have their own unique fragrance. Note the subtle differences between smells from different parts of the body and what effect they have on you. Women: if your lover is aroused by genital scent, use it like perfume, rubbing your vaginal juices on your neck and chest. In one study, women who did this said that their lovers suddenly sat up and took much more notice of them sexually.

smell

64 Fill the bath with hot water and sprinkle rose petals on the top. Now wash and shampoo each other. When you're dry, rub fruit-scented body lotion all over each other's skin.

65 Give each other a head-to-toe aromatherapy massage using a ready-made massage oil. Choose one with aphrodisiac qualities, such as ylang ylang, neroli, jasmine or sandalwood.

66 A familiar scent that you associate with your lover can trigger memories – and instant arousal. Stay connected when you're apart by keeping a piece of clothing imbued with "their smell".

Good sex comes with its own sound effects. Nothing quite compares to the involuntary sounds of your lover responding to your touch. Knowing this, it's important to relax and be as vocal as you like during sex. (But there's also something deliciously naughty about being forced to make love in silence just in case someone hears you — for example, in a bathroom at a party.) The next best thing to hearing the sighs, pants, moans and groans of your lover in bed is the sound of their voice sound

describing all the things that they're going to do to you, so don't flinch from talking dirty. The rules of erotic talk are: first, match your voice to the rhythm of sex by speeding up, slowing down, getting breathless and including pauses in which you do nothing but breathe passionately. Second, use language that your lover uses in bed and steer clear of unsexy medical terms. Third, relax and sound like you're really enjoying it. If *you* get turned on, your lover will too – arousal is infectious.

67 Get intimate by dancing together to a recording of African drumming. Don't worry about how you look – just abandon yourselves wholeheartedly to the intoxicating rhythmns.

68 Try having sex
to loud music.
Although lovers often
make love to slow,
romantic songs, research
shows that many of us
are more turned on by
rhythmic, pumping beats.

69 Read with your lover in bed. Choose one of your favourite erotic stories and take turns reading passages from it out loud in your sexiest and most seductive voices.